NATIONAL GEOGRAPHIC

Ladders

Common Core Readers

Birthday Celebrations

GENRE Social Studies Article

Read to find out how people celebrate birthdays.

International

by Elizabeth Gilbert | illustrations by Leslie Harrington

"Happy Birthday!" Around the World

People all over the world speak different languages. They also have special greetings for important events, such as birthdays. Here is how people say "Happy Birthday" in ten languages from around the world.

Happy Birthday
(HA-peeh BERTH-day)
English

Janmadin mubarak ho
(jahn-mah-DIN moo-BAH-rahk HOH)
Hindi

Alles gute zum Geburtstag
(AH-les goot zoom geh-BURS-tahg)
German

S'dniom roshedenea
(s dnyom rozh-DEE-nyah)
Russian

Birthday Bash

Feliz cumpleaños
(fay-LEES coom-plee-AHN-yohs)
Spanish

Maligayang kaarawan
(maah-lee-GAH-yang kah-AH-rah-wahn)
Tagalog

Kule sana wintie tayyiba (to a girl)
(koo-LEH SAH-na win-TEE tie-EE-bah)
Arabic (in Egypt)

Kule sana winta tayib (to a boy)
(koo-LEH SAH-na win-TAH TIE-eeb)
Arabic (in Egypt)

Otanjobi omedeto gozaimasu
(oh-tan-JOH-bee oh-med-ih-toh goh-zah-ee-mas)
Japanese

Feliz Aniversário
(fay-LEEZ ah-nee-vair-SAH-ree-yoh)
Portuguese

Sheng ri kuai le
(shung-rur KWAI-luh)
Mandarin

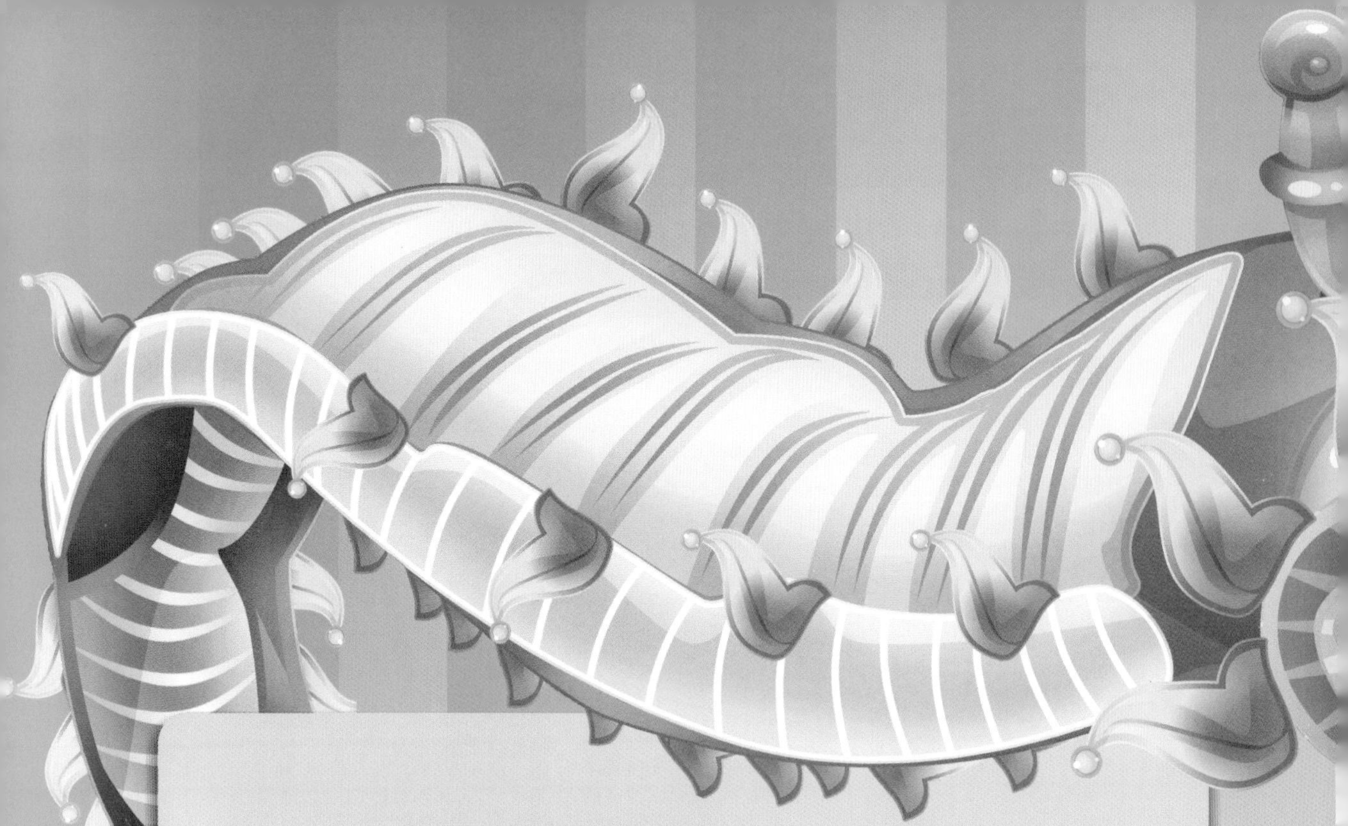

Birthday Traditions

Picture your family and friends smiling, talking, and listening to music you love. You are at your own birthday party. You are following a **tradition** that celebrates your life so far. But people have many ways of celebrating birthdays. Instead of a cake, picture a birthday pie on the table. What if paper flowers **decorated** your home? Or, what if your friends were getting ready to play *pusa at aso,* which means "cat and dog"?

In Canada, the United States, Egypt, and some European countries, it is popular to have cake with candles. This tradition began in Germany. Germans were famous for making beautiful candles. About 200 years ago, they began the tradition of arranging candles around birthday cakes. Years later Germans began putting candles on the cakes, and the birthday children made wishes and blew them out.

These objects are used in different birthday traditions. Read to find out more about these and other objects from around the world.

North America

In the United States and Canada, people often have similar birthday traditions. The birthday child invites friends and family to a party. The party room may be decorated with balloons. Guests may give gifts and sing "Happy Birthday to You." After the song, the birthday child makes a wish and blows out all of the candles on the cake, which everyone then eats.

Piñata

Mexican children usually have *piñatas* at their birthday **celebrations.** People make *piñatas* or buy them at a store. *Piñatas* are often shaped like animals and filled with treats. Party guests hit the *piñata* with a stick. They want to break it open so they can grab the treats that will spill out. Many people in North and South America use *piñatas* at birthday parties and on other special **occasions.**

South America

Bunches of real or paper flowers at birthday parties in Brazil add to the fun. Chocolate bonbons, called *brigadeiros,* are a favorite treat. Colorful marzipan candies can look so beautiful and realistic that guests almost won't want to eat them!

In Peru, guests at birthday parties and other special events may get a handmade *recordatorio* pin. These pins are beautifully decorated. Party guests may save them for many years.

In Latin America, the *fiesta de quince años* is the most important **milestone** for a girl who is turning fifteen. The birthday girl wears a fancy dress and her first pair of high-heeled shoes as she dances with her father. This tradition may have begun hundreds of years ago in Mexico. Today the *fiesta de quince años* is also celebrated in Brazil, Ecuador, Paraguay, and many other countries.

Europe

In England birthday cakes may hide small objects, such as coins, buttons, and rings. A tradition says the objects can show a person his or her future. For example, a coin in your slice of birthday cake means you will have plenty of money when you are older. A button means the opposite—you will have less money. If you find a ring, it means you will get married one day.

In Switzerland parents might plant a fruit tree when a child is born. The parents hope that as the tree grows strong, their child will, too. The tradition is to plant an apple tree for a boy and a pear tree for a girl.

One German birthday tradition is to light a life candle at dinner and watch it burn down one notch. The family will light the life candle each year until the child turns 12.

Make Your Own Life Candle

What You Will Need

- 10-inch pillar candle
- Permanent marker
- Ruler
- Decorations

- Measure ¾ inch from the bottom of the candle and write 12.
- Measure and write numerals from 11 to 1 (from bottom to top). Each numeral should be ¾ inch apart.
- Decorate your candle with stars, stickers, sequins, glitter, and colorful shapes.

Africa

Some Egyptians like to have very large birthday parties. Two birthday cakes are needed so there is enough cake for all of the guests! They put candles on only one cake, however. Egyptians also eat small sandwiches and other snacks at birthday parties.

Children in Ghana have a special birthday breakfast called *oto* (AH-toh). It is made from eggs and sweet potatoes. Then, at birthday parties, Ghanaian children eat other traditional foods, such as fried plantains.

Zulu birthday parties involve eating, singing, and dancing. Zulus do not send out formal invitations. It is considered an honor to the birthday person when guests show up uninvited.

Asia

Chinese New Year is the occasion to celebrate everyone's birthday. When a Chinese baby is born, he or she will be one year old at the following Chinese New Year. This happens even if the baby has not yet lived for one full year.

Hard-boiled eggs are dyed red for Chinese New Year.

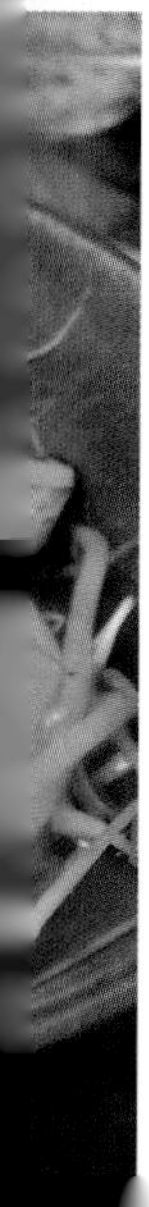

People from many Asian **cultures** eat long noodles at birthday parties. The noodles **symbolize** long life for the birthday person. The noodles must be swallowed whole, according to the tradition. Koreans eat traditional long-noodle dishes called *memil guksu* and *milguksu*.

Shichi-go-san is a Japanese holiday that honors girls who are turning three or seven and boys who are turning three or five.

Oceania

Pusa at aso, or "cat and dog," is a birthday party game played in the Philippines. The "dog" sits in the middle of a circle and protects its "bones." The "cats" sit in a circle around the dog and try to take the bones away from the dog without getting tagged.

One traditional party food in Australia is called hundreds-and-thousands bread. You can make it by spreading butter on bread and putting colored sprinkles on top.

Pass the Parcel is a popular party game in New Zealand. It is also popular in England, Nigeria, and other countries. Players sit in a circle. When music starts, they pass around a gift wrapped in layers of colored tissue paper. Smaller gifts are wrapped between each layer. When the music stops, the player holding the parcel removes one layer and keeps the gift inside.

New Traditions

A birthday with family and friends can be so much fun! People all over the world celebrate the occasion with games, food, and ceremonies. When your next birthday comes around, think about how other cultures celebrate. Then try a new tradition in honor of your very own new year.

Check In What makes a birthday celebration a tradition?

Read to find out how to make a colorful birthday cake.

How to Make a Rainbow Cake

by Emily Brown

For many people, birthday cake is one of the most important parts of any birthday **celebration.** Think about the cakes you've seen at birthday parties. Birthday cakes are often chocolate or yellow cake with chocolate or white frosting. Sometimes the cake is **decorated** with a birthday greeting or pictures of animals and flowers. The frosting on the outside may look fancy, but the cake underneath is just plain brown or yellow.

Why not make your birthday cake as interesting on the inside as it is on the outside? Start a new **tradition** and make a rainbow cake! On the following pages is an easy recipe you and an adult can follow. Before you begin, check to see if you have all of the **ingredients** in the recipe.

Ingredients

White cake mix

White cake frosting

Vegetable oil

Eggs

Food coloring

Directions

1 Follow the directions on the box of cake mix to make the cake **batter**.

2 Pour the cake batter into six small bowls.

3 Add red food coloring to the first bowl. Add blue to the second bowl. Add yellow to the third bowl.

4 Make three more colors in the remaining three bowls. Combine equal amounts of red and blue to make purple. Combine red and yellow to make orange. Combine yellow and blue to make green. Then mix the food coloring into the batter. Use a different spoon for each color.

5 Grease and flour a cake pan. Ask an adult to preheat the oven according to the directions on the box of cake mix.

6 Pour the first color of batter into the center of the pan. Slowly pour a different color on top of the first one. If you start with a dark color, use a light color next. Repeat for each color.

7 Have an adult bake the cake according to the instructions on the box of cake mix. Then frost the cake. Decorate it with sprinkles, candy, or whatever you wish.

Blow out the candles on your birthday cake and try a slice. Enjoy this special **occasion**. Every color of the rainbow is in your mouth!

Check In How is rainbow cake different from other birthday cake?

Discuss Text and Pictures

1. What do you think connects the two pieces that you read in this book? What makes you think that?

2. Choose a birthday tradition. Tell how the photos or pictures give you more information.

3. In "How to Make a Rainbow Cake," why is it important to follow the steps in order? How do the photos help?

4. What connections do you have to birthday celebrations? What questions do you still have after reading?